Merry Christmas

ISBN 978-1-4803-4555-3

HAL•LEONARD® CORPORATION

7777 W. BLUEMOUND RD. P.O. BOX 13819 MILWAUKEE, WI 53213

In Australia Contact:
Hal Leonard Australia Pty. Ltd.
4 Lentara Court
Cheltenham, Victoria, 3192 Australia
Email: ausadmin@halleonard.com.au

Visit Hal Leonard Online at
www.halleonard.com

GUITAR NOTATION LEGEND

THE MUSICAL STAFF shows pitches and rhythms and is divided by bar lines into measures. Pitches are named after the first seven letters of the alphabet.

TABLATURE graphically represents the guitar fingerboard. Each horizontal line represents a string, and each number represents a fret.

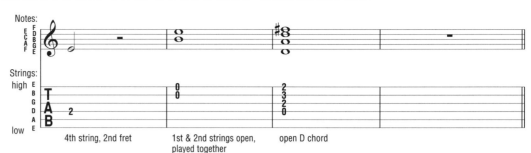

4th string, 2nd fret   1st & 2nd strings open, played together   open D chord

HALF-STEP BEND: Strike the note and bend up 1/2 step.

WHOLE-STEP BEND: Strike the note and bend up one step.

GRACE NOTE BEND: Strike the note and immediately bend up as indicated.

SLIGHT (MICROTONE) BEND: Strike the note and bend up 1/4 step.

BEND AND RELEASE: Strike the note and bend up as indicated, then release back to the original note. Only the first note is struck.

PRE-BEND: Bend the note as indicated, then strike it.

VIBRATO: The string is vibrated by rapidly bending and releasing the note with the fretting hand.

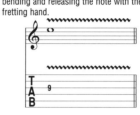

PALM MUTING: The note is partially muted by the pick hand lightly touching the string(s) just before the bridge.

HAMMER-ON: Strike the first (lower) note with one finger, then sound the higher note (on the same string) with another finger by fretting it without picking.

PULL-OFF: Place both fingers on the notes to be sounded. Strike the first note and without picking, pull the finger off to sound the second (lower) note.

LEGATO SLIDE: Strike the first note and then slide the same fret-hand finger up or down to the second note. The second note is not struck.

SHIFT SLIDE: Same as legato slide, except the second note is struck.

TRILL: Very rapidly alternate between the notes indicated by continuously hammering on and pulling off.

TAPPING: Hammer ("tap") the fret indicated with the pick-hand index or middle finger and pull off to the note fretted by the fret hand.

NATURAL HARMONIC: Strike the note while the fret-hand lightly touches the string directly over the fret indicated.

PINCH HARMONIC: The note is fretted normally and a harmonic is produced by adding the edge of the thumb or the tip of the index finger of the pick hand to the normal pick attack.

TREMOLO PICKING: The note is picked as rapidly and continuously as possible.

VIBRATO BAR DIVE AND RETURN: The pitch of the note or chord is dropped a specified number of steps (in rhythm), then returned to the original pitch.

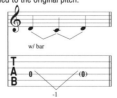

VIBRATO BAR SCOOP: Depress the bar just before striking the note, then quickly release the bar.

VIBRATO BAR DIP: Strike the note and then immediately drop a specified number of steps, then release back to the original pitch.

Additional Musical Definitions

(accent)   • Accentuate note (play it louder).

(staccato)   • Play the note short.

D.S. al Coda   • Go back to the sign (𝄋), then play until the measure marked "**To Coda**," then skip to the section labelled "**Coda**."

D.C. al Fine   • Go back to the beginning of the song and play until the measure marked "**Fine**" (end).

Fill   • Label used to identify a brief melodic figure which is to be inserted into the arrangement.

N.C.   • Harmony is implied.

• Repeat measures between signs.

• When a repeated section has different endings, play the first ending only the first time and the second ending only the second time.

Away in a Manger

Words by John T. McFarland (v.3)
Music by James R. Murray

Verse
Moderately slow

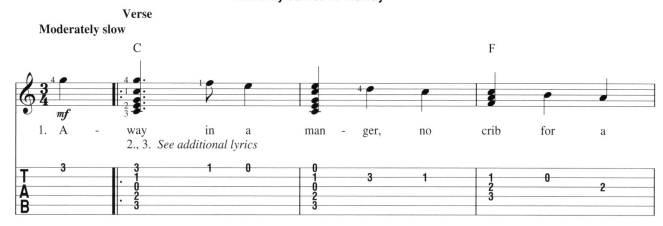

1. A - way in a man - ger, no crib for a
2., 3. *See additional lyrics*

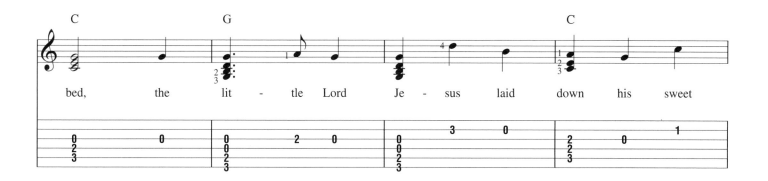

bed, the lit - tle Lord Je - sus laid down his sweet

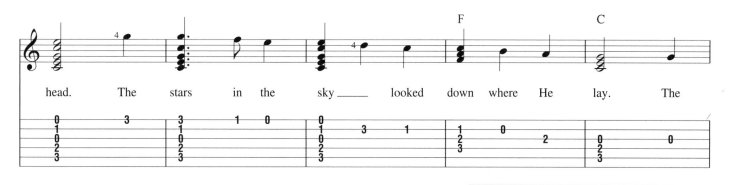

head. The stars in the sky _____ looked down where He lay. The

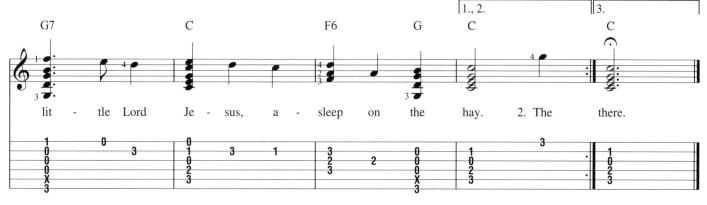

lit - tle Lord Je - sus, a - sleep on the hay. 2. The there.

Additional Lyrics

2. The cattle are lowing, the Baby awakes,
   But little Lord Jesus, no crying He makes.
   I love Thee, Lord Jesus, look down from the sky
   And stay by my cradle 'til morning is nigh.

3. Be near me, Lord Jesus, I ask Thee to stay
   Close by me forever, and love me, I pray.
   Bless all the dear children in Thy tender care,
   And fit us for heaven to live with Thee there.

Angels We Have Heard on High

Traditional French Carol
Translated by James Chadwick

Verse
Moderately

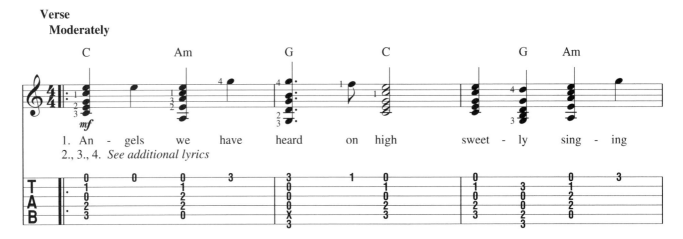

1. An - gels we have heard on high sweet - ly sing - ing
2., 3., 4. *See additional lyrics*

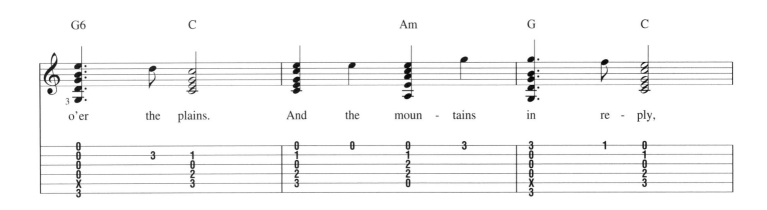

o'er the plains. And the moun - tains in re - ply,

Chorus

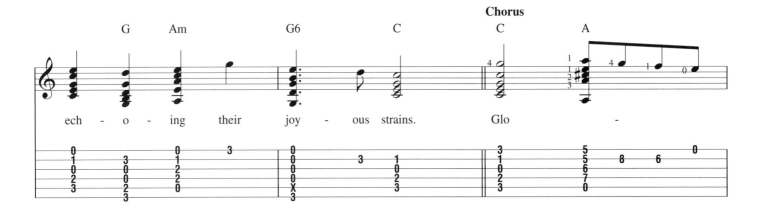

ech - o - ing their joy - ous strains. Glo -

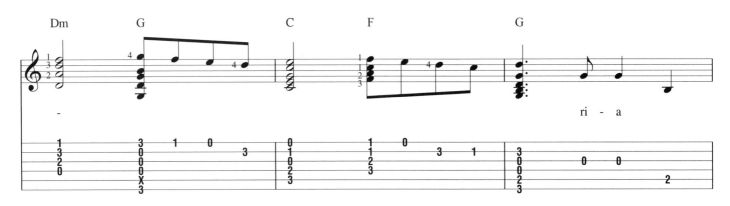

- ri - a

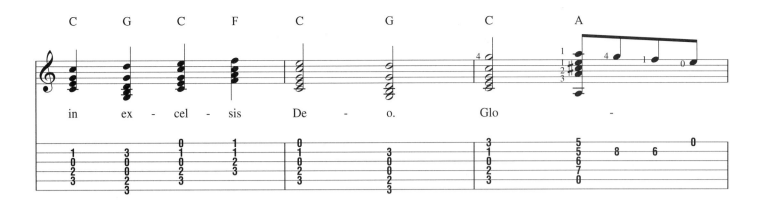

in ex - cel - sis De - o. Glo

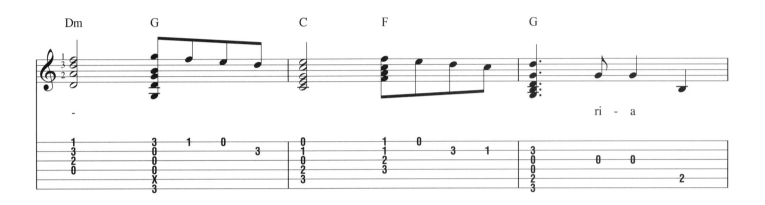

\- ri - a

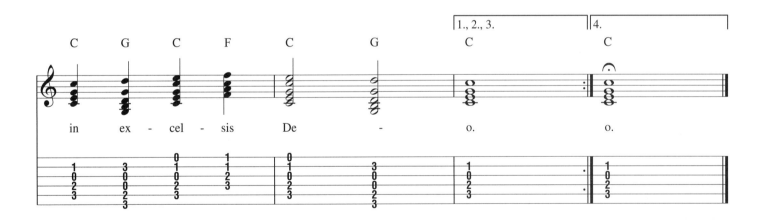

in ex - cel - sis De - o. o.

Additional Lyrics

2. Shepherds, why this jubilee? Why your joyous strains prolong?
   What the gladsome tidings be which inspire your heav'nly song?

3. Come to Bethlehem and see Him whose birth the angels sing;
   Come, adore on bended knee Christ the Lord, the newborn King.

4. See within a manger laid Jesus, Lord of heav'n and earth!
   Mary, Joseph, lend your aid, with us sing our Savior's birth.

Deck the Hall

Traditional Welsh Carol

Verse 1: Deck the hall with boughs of holly; fa, la, la, la, la, la, la, la, la.
2., 3. *See additional lyrics*

'Tis the season to be jolly; fa, la, la, la, la, la, la, la, la.

Don we now our gay apparel; fa, la, la, la, la, la, la, la, la.

Troll the ancient Yuletide carol; fa, la, la, la, la, la, la, la, la. la, la, la.

Additional Lyrics

2. See the blazing yule before us;
   Fa, la, la, la, la, la, la, la, la.
   Strike the harp and join the chorus;
   Fa, la, la, la, la, la, la, la, la.
   Follow me in merry measure;
   Fa, la, la, la, la, la, la, la, la.
   While I tell of Yuletide treasure;
   Fa, la, la, la, la, la, la, la, la.

3. Fast away the old year passes;
   Fa, la, la, la, la, la, la, la, la.
   Hail the new ye lads and lasses;
   Fa, la, la, la, la, la, la, la, la.
   Sing we joyous, all together;
   Fa, la, la, la, la, la, la, la, la.
   Heedless of the wind and weather;
   Fa, la, la, la, la, la, la, la, la.

O Holy Night

French Words by Placide Cappeau
English Words by John S. Dwight
Music by Adolphe Adam

Verse
Slow, in 2

1. O ho - ly night, the stars are bright - ly shin - ing; it is the night of the dear Sav - ior's birth. Long lay the world in sin and er - ror pin - ing, 'til He ap - peared and the soul felt its worth. A Sweet

2. Tru - ly He taught us to love one an - oth - er. His law is love, and the His gos - pel is peace. Chains shall He break, for the slave is our broth - er, and in His name all op - pres - sion shall cease.

night... when Christ was born... O
ev - er - more was pro - claim! His

1.
night, ... O ho - ly

night, O night di - vine!

2.
pow'r ... and glo - ry

ev - er - more pro - claim!

The First Noël

17th Century English Carol
Music from W. Sandys' Christmas Carols

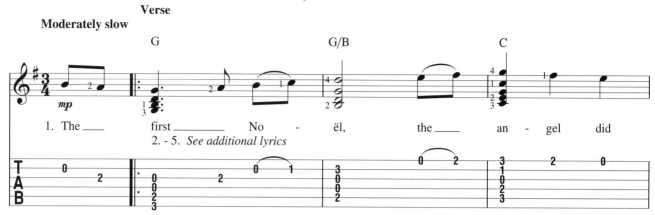

Verse
Moderately slow

1. The ___ first ___ No - ël, the ___ an - gel did
2. - 5. *See additional lyrics*

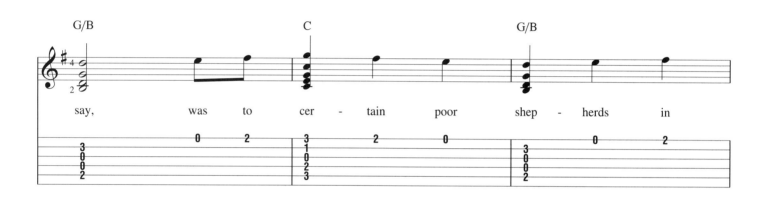

say, was to cer - tain poor shep - herds in

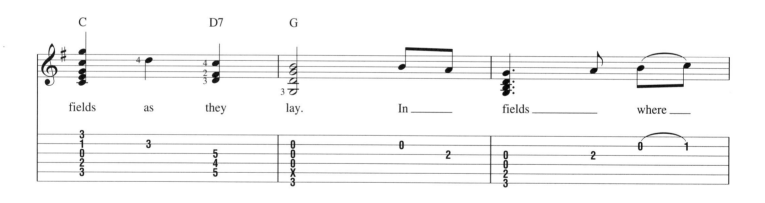

fields as they lay. In ___ fields ___ where ___

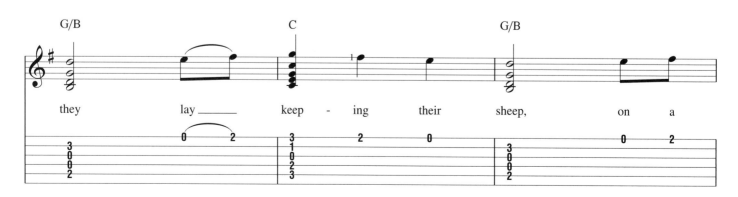

they lay ___ keep - ing their sheep, on a

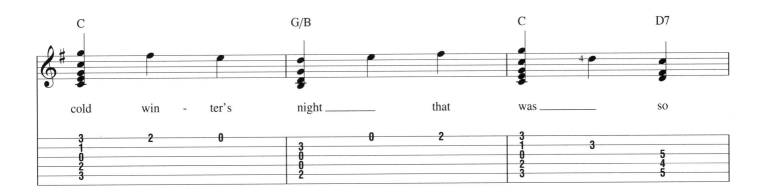

cold   win - ter's   night _____   that   was _____   so

Chorus

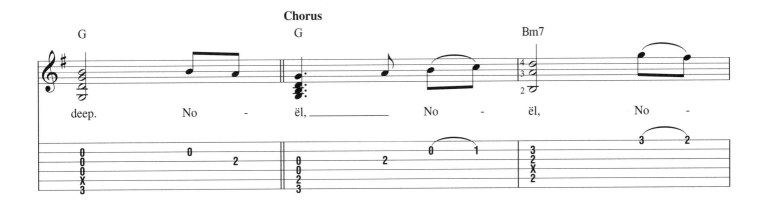

deep.   No - ël, _____   No - ël,   No -

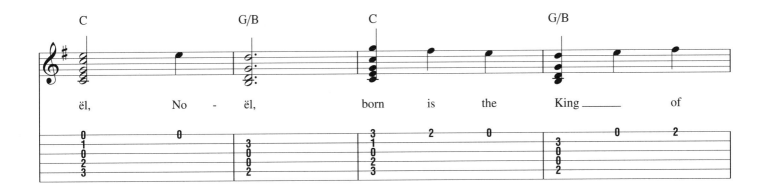

ël,   No - ël,   born   is   the   King _____   of

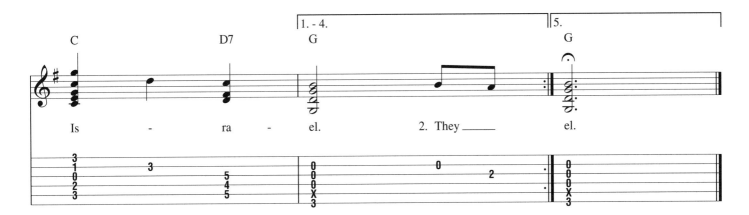

Is - ra - el.   2. They _____   el.

Additional Lyrics

2. They looked up and saw a star
   Shining in the east, beyond them far.
   And to the earth it gave great light
   And so it continued both day and night.

3. And by the light of that same star,
   Three wise men came from country far;
   To seek for a King was their intent,
   And to follow the star wherever it went.

4. This star drew nigh to the northwest,
   O'er Bethlehem it took its rest;
   And there it did both stop and stay,
   Right over the place where Jesus lay.

5. Then entered in those wise men three,
   Fell reverently upon their knee,
   And offered there in His presence,
   Their gold and myrrh and frankincense.

God Rest Ye Merry, Gentlemen

19th Century English Carol

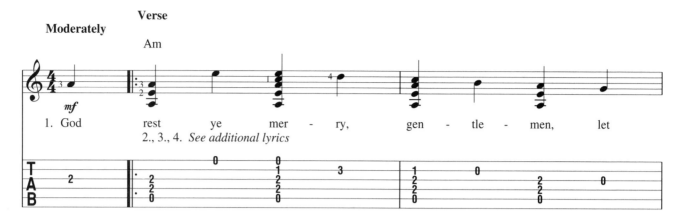

1. God rest ye mer - ry, gen - tle - men, let
2., 3., 4. *See additional lyrics*

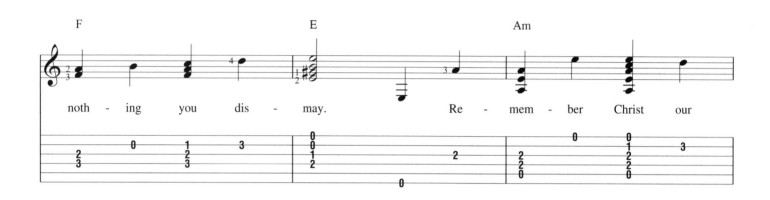

noth - ing you dis - may. Re - mem - ber Christ our

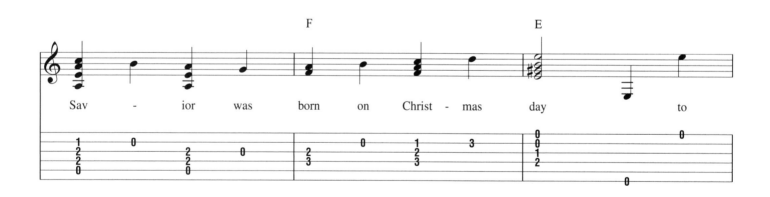

Sav - ior was born on Christ - mas day to

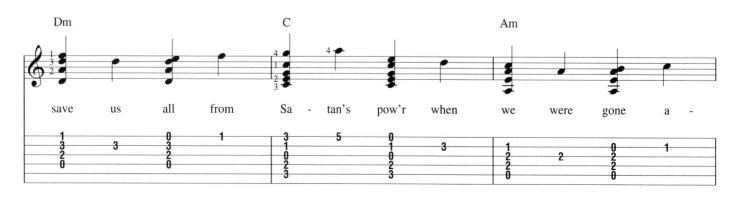

save us all from Sa - tan's pow'r when we were gone a -

Chorus

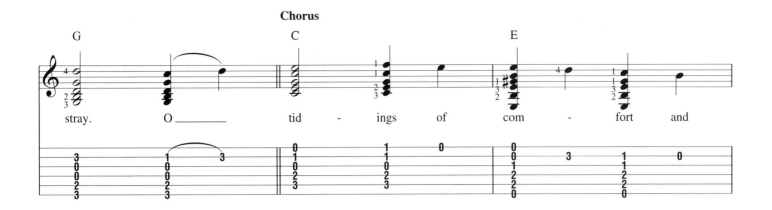

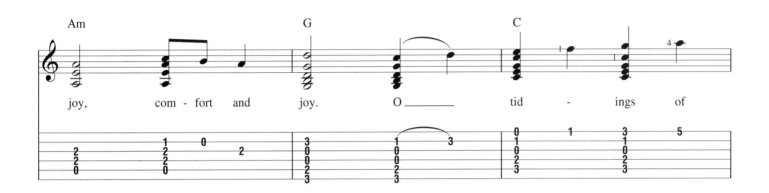

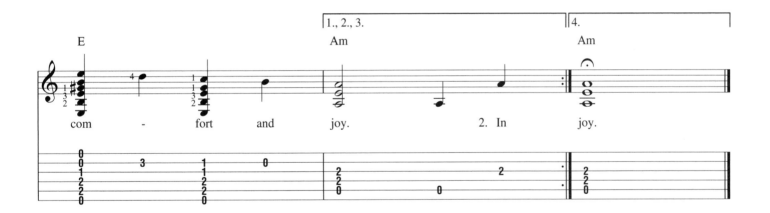

Additional Lyrics

2. In Bethlehem, in Jewry, this blessed Babe was born
   And laid within a manger upon this blessed morn
   That which His mother Mary did nothing take in scorn.

3. From God, our heav'nly Father, a blessed angel came
   And unto certain shepherds brought tidings of the same.
   How that in Bethlehem was born the Son of God by name.

4. Now shepherds, at those tidings, rejoiced much in mind
   And left their flocks a feeding in tempest, storm and wind
   And went to Bethlehem straightway the Son of God to find.

It Came Upon the Midnight Clear

Words by Edmund Hamilton Sears
Music by Richard Storrs Willis

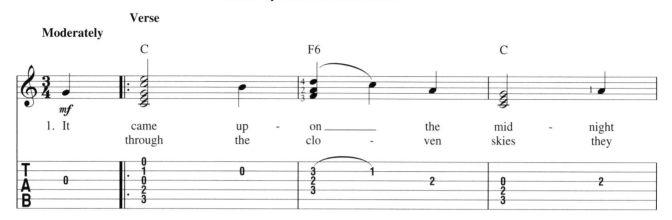

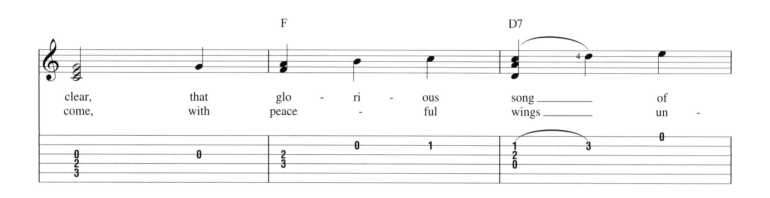

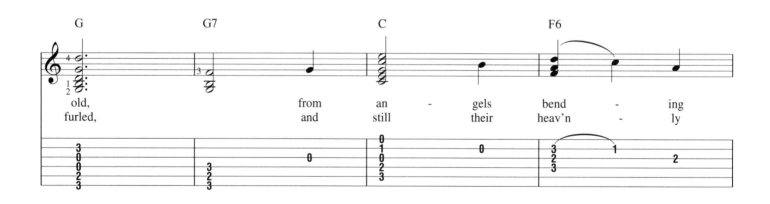

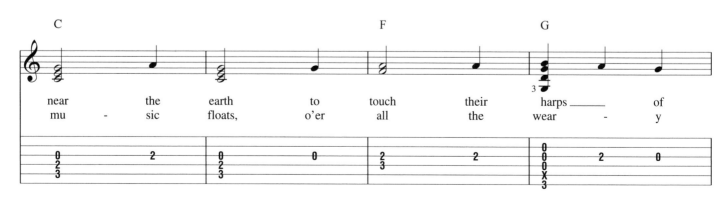

Jingle Bells

Words and Music by J. Pierpont

Verse
Moderately, in 2

1. Dash - ing through the snow in a one horse o - pen sleigh,
2., 3. *See additional lyrics*

O'er the fields we go, laugh - ing all the way.

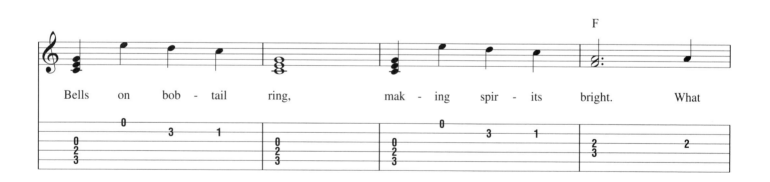

Bells on bob - tail ring, mak - ing spir - its bright. What

fun it is to ride and sing a sleigh - ing song to - night! Oh,

Chorus

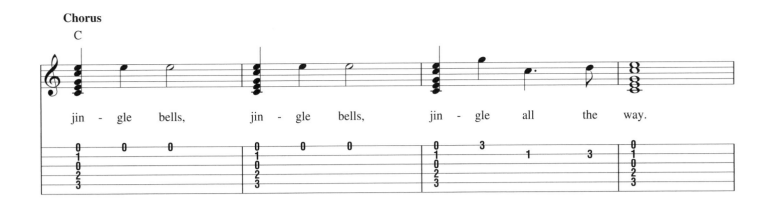

jin - gle bells, jin - gle bells, jin - gle all the way.

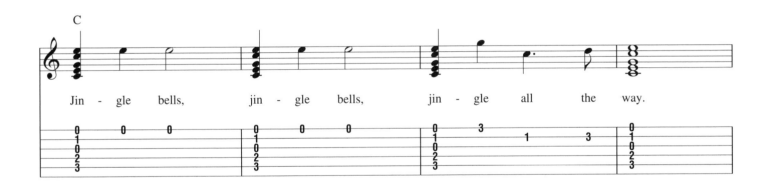

Oh, what fun it is to ride in a one horse o - pen sleigh! _____

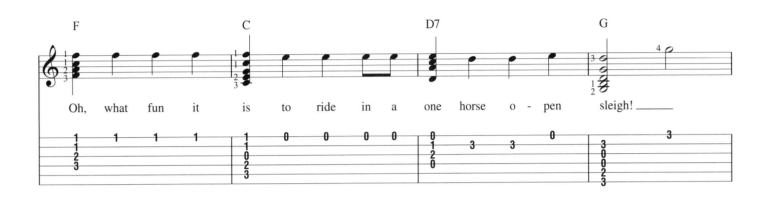

Jin - gle bells, jin - gle bells, jin - gle all the way.

Oh, what fun it is to ride in a one horse o - pen sleigh! 2. A sleigh!

Additional Lyrics

2. A day or two ago, I thought I'd take a ride,
   And soon Miss Fannie Bright was sitting by my side.
   The horse was lean and lank,
   Misfortune seemed his lot.
   He got into a drifted bank and we, we got upshot!

3. Now the ground is white, go it while you're young.
   Take the girls tonight and sing this sleighing song.
   Just get a bobtail bay, two-forty for his speed,
   Then hitch him to an open sleigh and
   Crack, you'll take the lead!

Joy to the World

Words by Isaac Watts
Music by George Frideric Handel
Adapted by Lowell Mason

Verse
Moderately slow, in 2

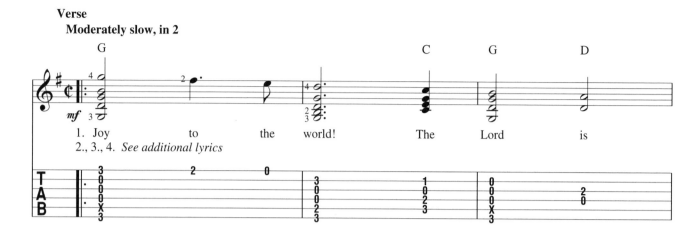

1. Joy to the world! The Lord is
2., 3., 4. *See additional lyrics*

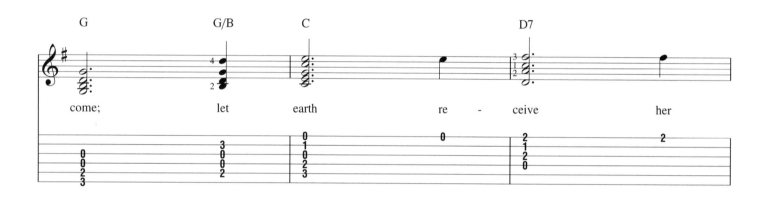

come; let earth re - ceive her

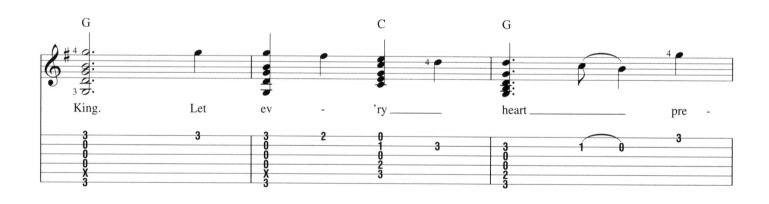

King. Let ev - 'ry _____ heart _____ pre -

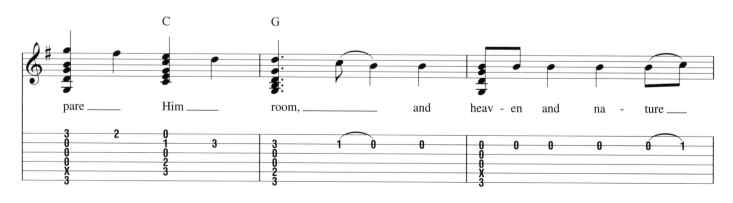

pare _____ Him _____ room, _____ and heav - en and na - ture _____

Lyrics: sing, and ___ heav - en and na - ture ___ sing, and ___

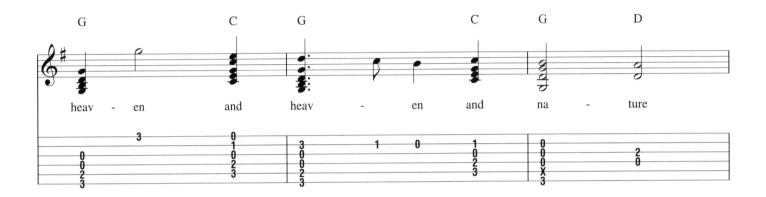

Lyrics: heav - en and heav - en and na - ture

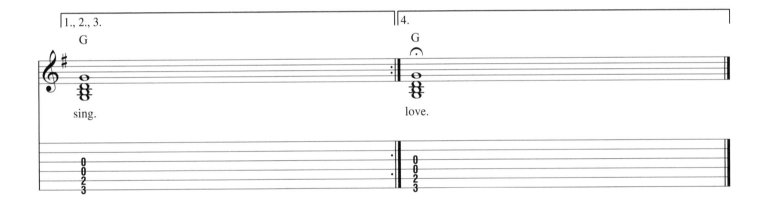

1., 2., 3. — sing.

4. — love.

Additional Lyrics

2. Joy to the world! The Savior reigns;
   Let men their songs employ
   While fields and floods,
   Rocks, hills and plains
   Repeat the sounding joy,
   Repeat the sounding joy,
   Repeat, repeat the sounding joy.

3. No more let sin and sorrow grow,
   Nor thorns infest the ground;
   He comes to make
   His blessings flow
   Far as the curse is found,
   Far as the curse is found,
   Far as, far as the curse is found.

4. He rules the world with truth and grace
   And makes the nations prove
   The glories of His righteousness
   And wonders of His love,
   And wonders of His love,
   And wonders, wonders of His love.

O Come, All Ye Faithful
(Adeste Fideles)

Music by John Francis Wade
Latin Words translated by Frederick Oakeley

Verse
Moderately

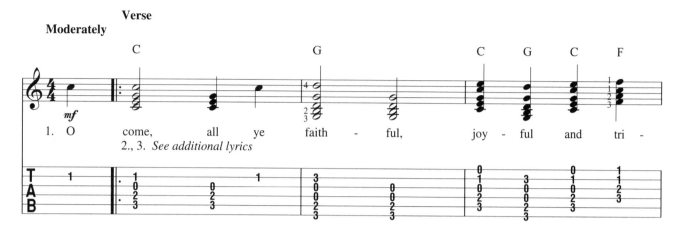

1. O come, all ye faith - ful, joy - ful and tri -
2., 3. *See additional lyrics*

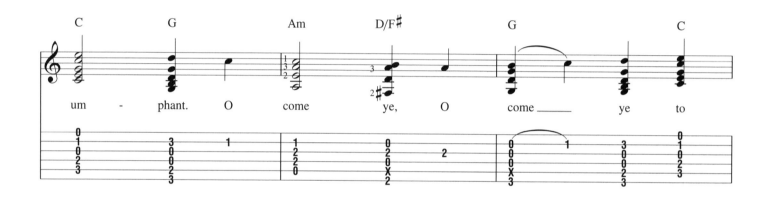

um - phant. O come ye, O come _____ ye to

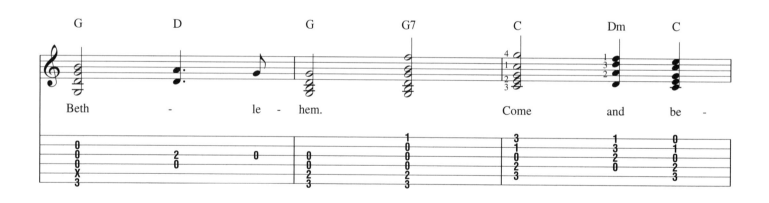

Beth - le - hem. Come and be -

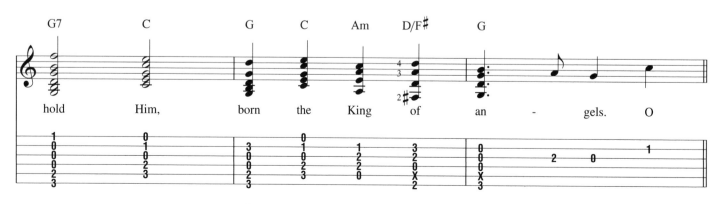

hold Him, born the King of an - gels. O

Chorus

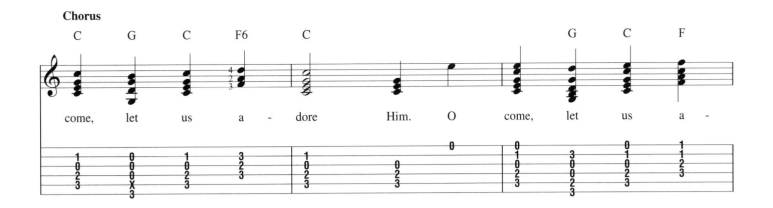

come, let us a - dore Him. O come, let us a -

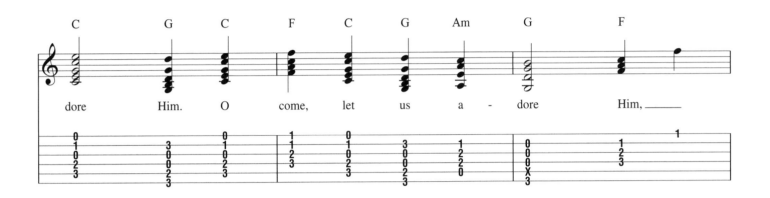

dore Him. O come, let us a - dore Him, _____

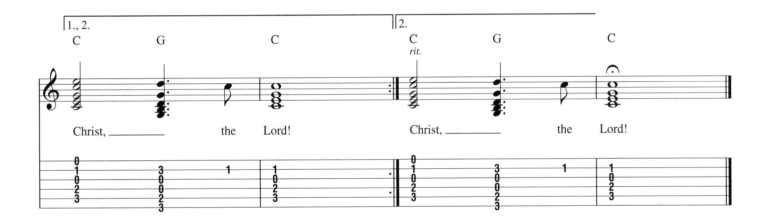

Christ, _____ the Lord! Christ, _____ the Lord!

Additional Lyrics

2. Sing choirs of angels, sing in exultation.
   O sing all ye citizens of heaven above.
   Glory to God in the highest.

3. Yea, Lord, we greet Thee, born this happy morning.
   Jesus, to Thee be all glory giv'n.
   Word of the Father, now in flesh appearing:

O Little Town of Bethlehem

Words by Phillips Brooks
Music by Lewis H. Redner

Additional Lyrics

2. For Christ is born of Mary, and gathered all above
While mortals sleep, the angels keep
Their watch of wond'ring love.
O morning stars, together proclaim the holy birth
And praises sing to God the King
And peace to men on earth!

3. O holy Child of Bethlehem, descend to us, we pray.
Cast out our sin and enter in;
Be born in us today.
We hear the Christmas angels the great glad tidings tell.
O come to us, abide with us
Our Lord, Immanuel!

We Wish You a Merry Christmas

Traditional English Folksong

Verse
Moderately

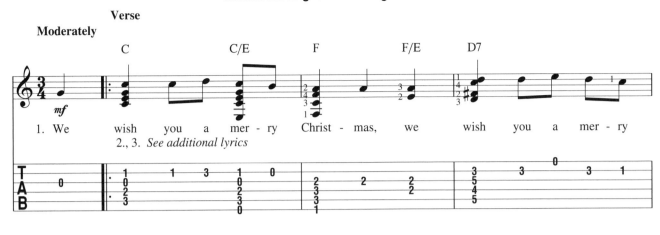

1. We wish you a mer - ry Christ - mas, we wish you a mer - ry
2., 3. *See additional lyrics*

Christ - mas, we wish you a mer - ry Christ - mas and a hap - py New

Bridge

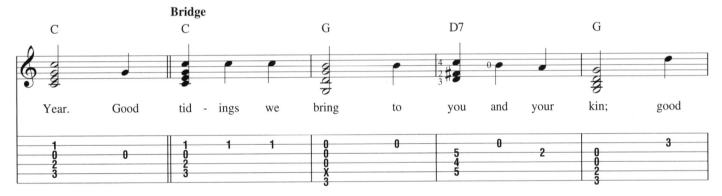

Year. Good tid - ings we bring to you and your kin; good

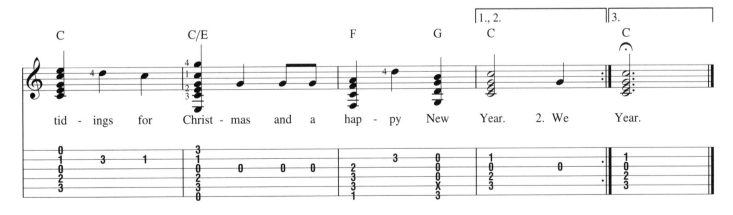

tid - ings for Christ - mas and a hap - py New Year. 2. We Year.

Additional Lyrics

2. We all want some figgy pudding,
   We all want some figgy pudding,
   We all want some figgy pudding,
   So bring some right here.

3. We won't go until we get some,
   We won't go until we get some,
   We won't go until we get some,
   So bring some right here.

Silent Night

Words by Joseph Mohr
Translated by John F. Young
Music by Franz X. Gruber

Verse
Moderately slow

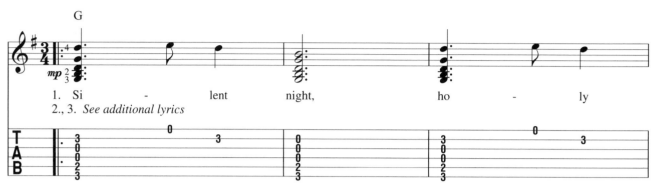

1. Si - lent night, ho - ly
2., 3. *See additional lyrics*

night! All is calm, all is

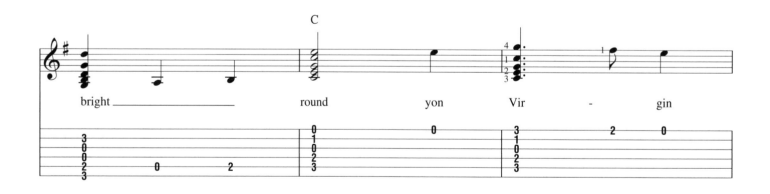

bright _____ round yon Vir - gin

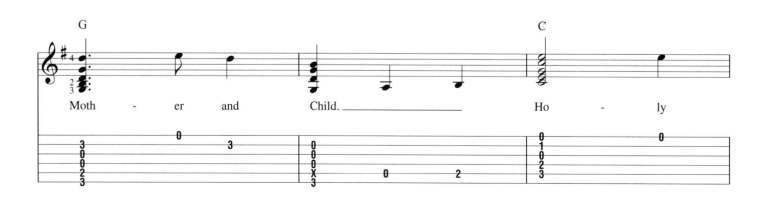

Moth - er and Child. _____ Ho - ly

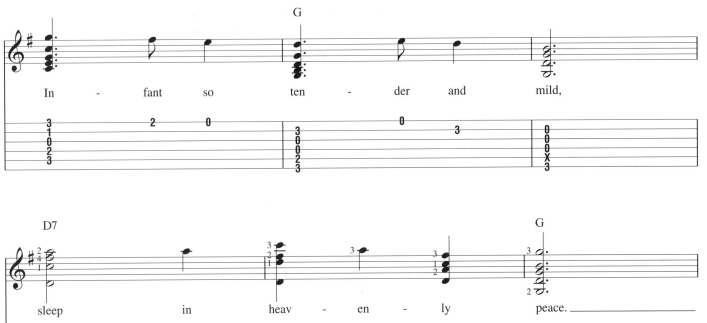

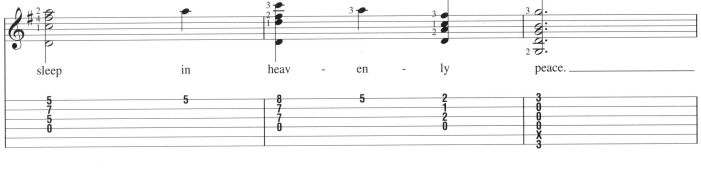

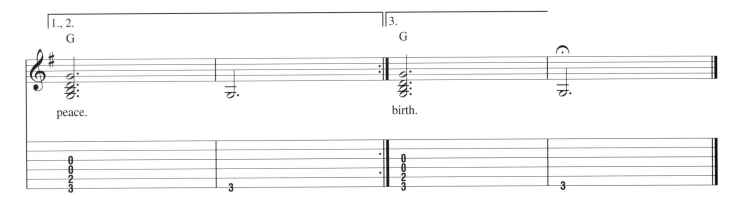

Additional Lyrics

2. Silent night, holy night!
Shepherds quake at the sight.
Glories stream from heaven afar.
Heavenly hosts sing Alleluia.
Christ the Savior is born!
Christ the Savior is born!

3. Silent night, holy night!
Son of God, love's pure light.
Radiant beams from thy holy face
With the dawn of redeeming grace.
Jesus, Lord at Thy birth.
Jesus, Lord at Thy birth.

We Three Kings of Orient Are

Words and Music by John H. Hopkins, Jr.

Verse
Moderately fast

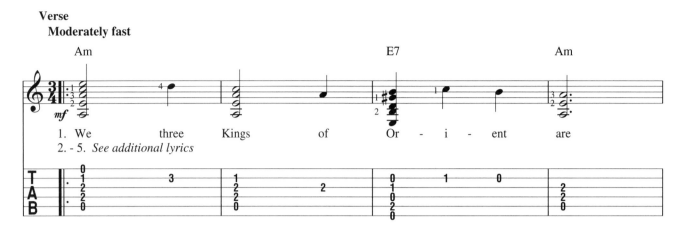

1. We three Kings of Or - i - ent are
2. - 5. *See additional lyrics*

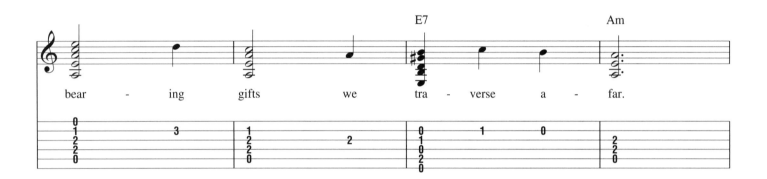

bear - ing gifts we tra - verse a - far.

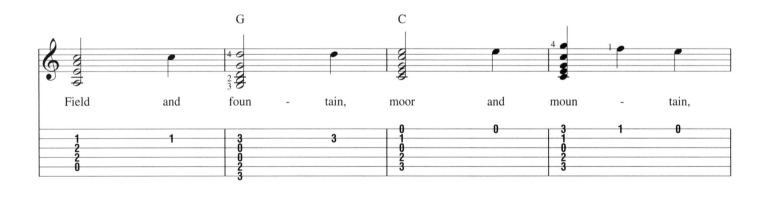

Field and foun - tain, moor and moun - tain,

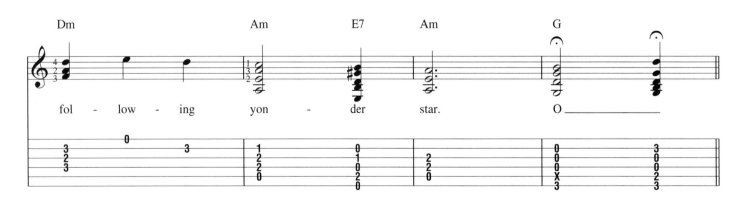

fol - low - ing yon - der star. O _____

Chorus

star of won - der, star of night, star with
roy - al beau - ty bright, west - ward
lead - ing, still pro - ceed - ing, guide us
to thy per - fect light. light.

Additional Lyrics

2. Born a King on Bethlehem plain,
   Gold I bring to crown Him again.
   King forever, ceasing never,
   Over us all to reign.

3. Frankincense to offer have I;
   Incense owns a Deity nigh;
   Prayer and praising, all men raising,
   Worship Him, God most high.

4. Myrrh us mine; it's bitter perfume
   Breathes a life of gathering gloom;
   Sorrowing, sighing, bleeding, dying;
   Sealed in the stone-cold tomb.

5. Glorious now, behold Him arise,
   King and God, and Sacrifice!
   Heav'n sings alleluia,
   Alleluia the earth replies:

What Child Is This?

Words by William C. Dix
16th Century English Melody

Verse
Moderately slow

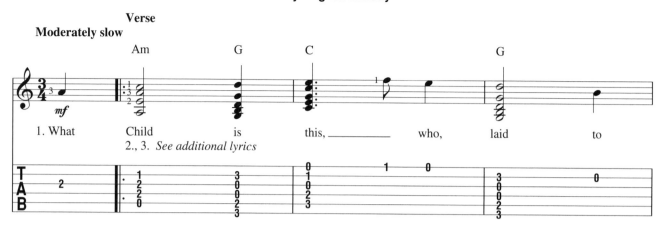

1. What Child is this, _____ who, laid to
2., 3. *See additional lyrics*

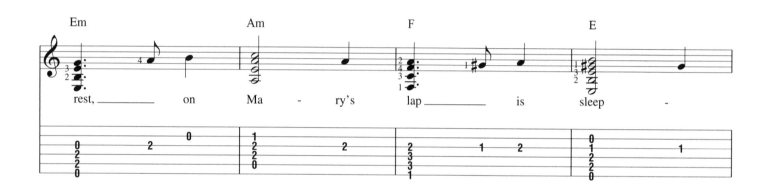

rest, _____ on Ma - ry's lap _____ is sleep -

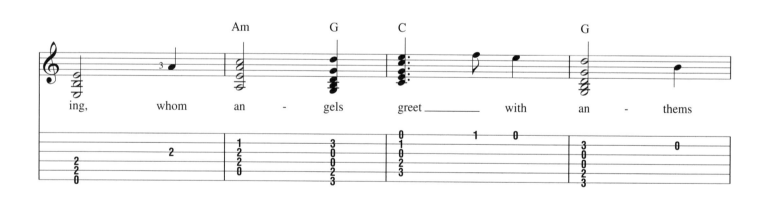

ing, whom an - gels greet _____ with an - thems

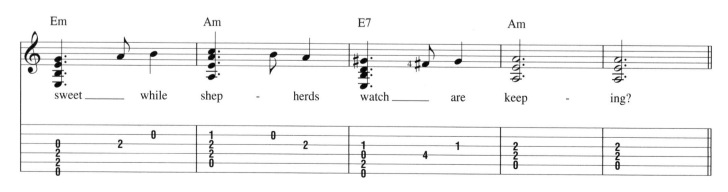

sweet _____ while shep - herds watch _____ are keep - ing?

Chorus

Additional Lyrics

2. Why lies He in such mean estate where ox and ass are feeding?
   Good Christian, fear, for sinners here the silent Word is pleading.

3. So bring Him incense, gold, and myrrh; come peasant King, to own Him.
   The King of kings salvation brings; let loving hearts enthrone Him.

CELEBRATE CHRISTMAS
WITH YOUR GUITAR AND HAL LEONARD

THE BEST CHRISTMAS GUITAR FAKE BOOK EVER – 2ND EDITION

Over 150 Christmas classics for guitar. Songs include: Blue Christmas • The Chipmunk Song • Frosty the Snow Man • Happy Holiday • A Holly Jolly Christmas • I Saw Mommy Kissing Santa Claus • I Wonder As I Wander • Jingle-Bell Rock • Rudolph, the Red-Nosed Reindeer • Santa Bring My Baby Back (To Me) • Suzy Snowflake • Tennessee Christmas • and more.
00240053 Melody/Lyrics/Chords $19.95

THE BIG CHRISTMAS COLLECTION FOR EASY GUITAR

Includes over 70 Christmas favorites, such as: Ave Maria • Blue Christmas • Deck the Hall • Feliz Navidad • Frosty the Snow Man • Happy Holiday • A Holly Jolly Christmas • Joy to the World • O Holy Night • Silver and Gold • Suzy Snowflake • and more. Does not include TAB.
00698978 Easy Guitar $16.95

CHRISTMAS
Guitar Play-Along Volume 22
Book/CD Pack

8 songs: The Christmas Song (Chestnuts Roasting on an Open Fire) • Frosty the Snow Man • Happy Xmas (War Is Over) • Here Comes Santa Claus (Right Down Santa Claus Lane) • Jingle-Bell Rock • Merry Christmas, Darling • Rudolph the Red-Nosed Reindeer • Silver Bells.
00699600 Guitar Tab $15.95

CHRISTMAS CAROLS
Guitar Chord Songbook

80 favorite carols for guitarists who just need the lyrics and chords: Angels We Have Heard on High • Away in a Manger • Deck the Hall • Good King Wenceslas • The Holly and the Ivy • Irish Carol • Jingle Bells • Joy to the World • O Holy Night • Rocking • Silent Night • Up on the Housetop • Welsh Carol • What Child Is This? • and more.
00699536 Lyrics/Chord Symbols/Guitar Chord Diagrams $12.95

CHRISTMAS CAROLS
Guitar Play-Along Volume 62
Book/CD Pack

8 songs: God Rest Ye Merry, Gentlemen • Hark! The Herald Angels Sing • It Came upon the Midnight Clear • O Come, All Ye Faithful (Adeste Fideles) • O Holy Night • Silent Night • We Three Kings of Orient Are • What Child Is This?
00699798 Guitar Tab $12.95

CHRISTMAS CAROLS
Jazz Guitar Chord Melody Solos

Chord melody arrangements in notes & tab of 26 songs of the season. Includes: Auld Lang Syne • Deck the Hall • Good King Wenceslas • Here We Come A-Wassailing • Joy to the World • O Little Town of Bethlehem • Toyland • We Three Kings of Orient Are • and more.
00701697 Solo Guitar $12.99

CHRISTMAS SONGS
Guitar Chord Songbook

80 Christmas favorites, including: Baby, It's Cold Outside • The Chipmunk Song • The Christmas Shoes • The Christmas Song • Grandma Got Run over by a Reindeer • Happy Holiday • I've Got My Love to Keep Me Warm • It Must Have Been the Mistletoe (Our First Christmas) • Miss You Most at Christmas Time • Silver Bells • We Need a Little Christmas • and more.
00699537 Lyrics/Chord Symbols/Guitar Chord Diagrams $12.95

CLASSICAL GUITAR CHRISTMAS COLLECTION

Includes classical guitar arrangements in standard notation and tablature for more than two dozen beloved carols: Angels We Have Heard on High • Auld Lang Syne • Ave Maria • Away in a Manger • Canon in D • The First Noel • I Saw Three Ships • Joy to the World • O Christmas Tree • O Holy Night • Silent Night • What Child Is This? • and more.
00699493 Guitar Solo $9.95

FINGERPICKING CHRISTMAS

Features 20 classic carols for the intermediate-level guitarist. Includes: Away in a Manger • Deck the Hall • The First Noel • It Came upon the Midnight Clear • Jingle Bells • O Come, All Ye Faithful • Silent Night • We Wish You a Merry Christmas • What Child Is This? • and more.
00699599 Solo Guitar $8.95

FINGERPICKING CHRISTMAS CLASSICS

15 favorite holiday tunes, with each solo combining melody and harmony in one superb fingerpicking arrangement. Includes: Christmas Time Is Here • Feliz Navidad • I Saw Mommy Kissing Santa Claus • Mistletoe and Holly • My Favorite Things • Santa Baby • Somewhere in My Memory • and more.
00701695 Solo Guitar $7.99

FINGERPICKING YULETIDE

Carefully written for intermediate-level guitarists, this collection includes an introduction to fingerstyle guitar and 16 holiday favorites: Do You Hear What I Hear • Happy Xmas (War Is Over) • A Holly Jolly Christmas • Jingle-Bell Rock • Rudolph the Red-Nosed Reindeer • and more.
00699654 Fingerstyle Guitar $9.99

THE ULTIMATE CHRISTMAS GUITAR SONGBOOK

100 songs in a variety of notation styles, from easy guitar and classical guitar arrangements to note-for-note guitar tab transcriptions. Includes: All Through the Night • Auld Lang Syne • Away in a Manger • Blue Christmas • The Chipmunk Song • The Gift • I've Got My Love to Keep Me Warm • Jingle Bells • One Bright Star • Santa Baby • Silver Bells • Wonderful Christmastime • and more.
00700185 Multi-Arrangements $19.95

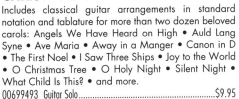
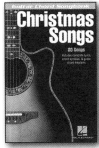
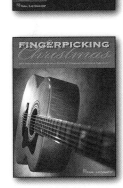

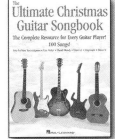

FOR MORE INFORMATION, SEE YOUR LOCAL MUSIC DEALER, OR WRITE TO:

HAL•LEONARD® CORPORATION
7777 W. BLUEMOUND RD. P.O. BOX 13819 MILWAUKEE, WI 53213

www.halleonard.com

Prices, contents and availability subject to change without notice.

0711

JAZZ GUITAR CHORD MELODY SOLOS

This series features chord melody arrangements in standard notation and tablature of songs for intermediate guitarists.

"Well-crafted arrangements that sound great and are still accessible to most players."
– *Guitar Edge* magazine

ALL-TIME STANDARDS [INCLUDES TAB]
27 songs, including: All of Me • Bewitched • Come Fly with Me • A Fine Romance • Georgia on My Mind • How High the Moon • I'll Never Smile Again • I've Got You Under My Skin • It's De-Lovely • It's Only a Paper Moon • My Romance • Satin Doll • The Surrey with the Fringe on Top • Yesterdays • and more.
00699757 Solo Guitar $14.99

CHRISTMAS CAROLS [INCLUDES TAB]
26 songs, including: Auld Lang Syne • Away in a Manger • Deck the Hall • God Rest Ye Merry, Gentlemen • Good King Wenceslas • Here We Come A-Wassailing • It Came upon the Midnight Clear • Joy to the World • O Holy Night • O Little Town of Bethlehem • Silent Night • Toyland • We Three Kings of Orient Are • and more.
00701697 Solo Guitar $12.99

DISNEY SONGS [INCLUDES TAB]
27 songs, including: Beauty and the Beast • Can You Feel the Love Tonight • Candle on the Water • Colors of the Wind • A Dream Is a Wish Your Heart Makes • Heigh-Ho • Some Day My Prince Will Come • Under the Sea • When You Wish upon a Star • A Whole New World (Aladdin's Theme) • Zip-A-Dee-Doo-Dah • and more.
00701902 Solo Guitar $14.99

DUKE ELLINGTON [INCLUDES TAB]
25 songs, including: C-Jam Blues • Caravan • Do Nothin' Till You Hear from Me • Don't Get Around Much Anymore • I Got It Bad and That Ain't Good • I'm Just a Lucky So and So • In a Sentimental Mood • It Don't Mean a Thing (If It Ain't Got That Swing) • Mood Indigo • Perdido • Prelude to a Kiss • Satin Doll • and more.
00700636 Solo Guitar $12.99

FAVORITE STANDARDS [INCLUDES TAB]
27 songs, including: All the Way • Autumn in New York • Blue Skies • Cheek to Cheek • Don't Get Around Much Anymore • How Deep Is the Ocean • I'll Be Seeing You • Isn't It Romantic? • It Could Happen to You • The Lady Is a Tramp • Moon River • Speak Low • Take the "A" Train • Willow Weep for Me • Witchcraft • and more.
00699756 Solo Guitar $14.99

FINGERPICKING JAZZ STANDARDS [INCLUDES TAB]
15 songs: Autumn in New York • Body and Soul • Can't Help Lovin' Dat Man • Easy Living • A Fine Romance • Have You Met Miss Jones? • I'm Beginning to See the Light • It Could Happen to You • My Romance • Stella by Starlight • Tangerine • The Very Thought of You • The Way You Look Tonight • When Sunny Gets Blue • Yesterdays.
00699840 Solo Guitar $7.99

JAZZ BALLADS [INCLUDES TAB]
27 songs, including: Body and Soul • Darn That Dream • Easy to Love (You'd Be So Easy to Love) • Here's That Rainy Day • In a Sentimental Mood • Misty • My Foolish Heart • My Funny Valentine • The Nearness of You • Stella by Starlight • Time After Time • The Way You Look Tonight • When Sunny Gets Blue • and more.
00699755 Solo Guitar $14.99

JAZZ CLASSICS [INCLUDES TAB]
27 songs, including: Blue in Green • Bluesette • Bouncing with Bud • Cast Your Fate to the Wind • Con Alma • Doxy • Epistrophy • Footprints • Giant Steps • Invitation • Lullaby of Birdland • Lush Life • A Night in Tunisia • Nuages • Ruby, My Dear • St. Thomas • Stolen Moments • Waltz for Debby • Yardbird Suite • and more.
00699758 Solo Guitar $14.99

Prices, content, and availability subject to change without notice. | Disney characters and artwork ©Disney Enterprises, Inc.

HAL•LEONARD®
www.halleonard.com